# WORLD WAR

## WAR AT

# SEA

# WORLD WAR II STORIES
# WAR AT
# SEA

# ANTHONY MASTERS

Illustrated by Joyce Macdonald

# W
## FRANKLIN WATTS
### LONDON•SYDNEY

**Editors** Belinda Hollyer, Louisa Sladen
**Editor-in-Chief** John C. Miles
**Design** Billin Design Solutions
**Art Director** Jonathan Hair

First published in 2004
by Franklin Watts
96 Leonard Street
London
EC2A 4XD

Franklin Watts Australia
45-51 Huntley Street
Alexandria
NSW 2015

ISBN 0 7496 4803 1

A CIP catalogue record for this book is available
from the British Library.

Printed in Great Britain

# CONTENTS

# PROLOGUE

## The Second World War

The German leader, Adolf Hitler, had swept to power in 1933. Hitler's Nazi Party planned to dominate Europe, and they soon built up their military strength. When Germany invaded the Rhineland, Austria and Czechoslovakia, no other countries opposed them. But then the German army rolled into Poland. The Allies, led by Britain and France, decided they must act. They wanted to halt the invasion of German forces throughout Europe. On 3 September 1939, Britain and France declared war on Germany.

At first, the war went badly for the Allies. By June 1940, France had been defeated by Germany. The British Expeditionary Force (BEF) had been in France, fighting with the

French against the Germans. Now the BEF was forced to retreat to the town of Dunkirk on the French coast.

While German aircraft bombed the helpless British soldiers, a desperate radio appeal was made to boat owners on the southern and eastern coasts of England. Anyone who could help was asked to sail across the English Channel to rescue British soldiers from Dunkirk. Hundreds of little boats made the dangerous journey under enemy fire, and 350,000 men were plucked from the beaches.

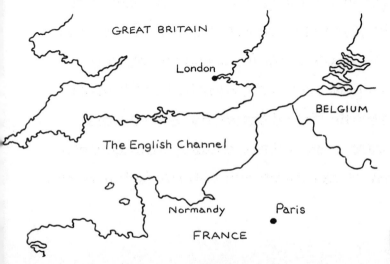

After the evacuation, the Germans were expected to invade Britain immediately. But Hitler made the wrong decision. He decided to delay the invasion until his forces had defeated Britain's Royal Air Force (RAF), and had conquered Russia.

But the RAF was not defeated. The Battle of Britain, in 1940, was fought and won in the air by British planes. In eastern Europe, Russia fiercely resisted the German invasion.

By 1941, the Allies realised just how important the war at sea was. If they could win that, they believed they could finally defeat Germany. The sea was a lifeline to Britain and its newest ally, Russia. Convoys of ships brought food, equipment and supplies across the Atlantic from Canada and the United States. But the convoys were under constant attack from German warships, aircraft and U-boats (submarines).

Japanese forces, fighting on Germany's side, attacked the American fleet at Pearl Harbor in December 1941. That brought the USA into the war on the Allied side. Now the sea war included the Pacific Ocean. American, Australian and New Zealand forces fought the Japanese in epic sea battles, trying to turn back their advance through Asia and the Pacific.

By June 1944, the Allies were doing well. The Allied commanders decided to invade Nazi-occupied Europe, and launched a bold attack on northern France. The success of the D-Day landings in June 1944 led to an Allied advance further into Europe, and the war in the Pacific continued. The Germans finally surrendered in May 1945, and the Japanese surrendered in September of the same year.

# THE HUNTING

During the Second World War, the war at sea put great pressure on Britain's Royal Navy. More ships were sunk, and more lives were lost, than in any previous war.

Norway, Denmark, the Netherlands, France and Belgium had all been defeated and occupied by the Nazis. That made the Royal Navy's task even more important. Britain had to be able to get vital food supplies through. Armies and equipment had to be moved. For the Allies to have a chance of winning the war, the sea lanes had to be kept open – somehow.

Ships travelled in convoys (groups) for protection. Most of the vessels in a convoy were unarmed merchant ships. These were guarded against attack by destroyers and corvettes (light, fast-moving warships).

Keith Langton was a midshipman (a junior officer) on board the destroyer HMS *Scorpion*. His ship took part in the convoys. They endured terrible weather conditions.

"Sometimes I thought the weather was on the enemy's side, with heaving, freezing cold seas, icebergs and dense patches of fog."

As Langton remembered: "We found ourselves in the Arctic, taking much-needed supplies to Russia, which was now [in 1941] under heavy attack by the Germans. Our hunters were German U-boats and battleships. Because of the fog we never knew whether they were suddenly going to appear."

U-boats might be lurking anywhere underneath icebergs. German battleships could use the fog as cover, and so move in on the convoy undetected.

The Arctic convoys began just after the Soviet Union (Russia) was invaded by Germany in 1941. Russia had been in an alliance with Germany, but now it joined the Allies. Then Britain offered help to the Russian leader, Josef Stalin. They set up supply routes between the two countries. But the Arctic routes were

NORWAY

very dangerous. The enemy was all around.
The Luftwaffe (the German air force), the
U-boats and the warships of the German
navy all lay in wait. And there were always
the icebergs, and the freezing fog, of the
Barents Sea.

*The location of the Barents Sea*
*and the northern Soviet Union.*

Arctic Ocean

Barents Sea

Tromso

Murmansk

LAPLAND

WEDEN

FINLAND

Arkhangelsk

SOVIET UNION

In fact, the *Scorpion* relied on storms and wild seas for protection, because those conditions kept the enemy at a distance. To deliver supplies to Russia and avoid enemy attack, the *Scorpion* had to sail across the Barents Sea in the Arctic.

Weather conditions were appalling in the Barents Sea. In winter the sun never rose, and so it was dark all the time. And it was so cold that the sailors got severe frostbite

if they ever went outside on to the top deck of the *Scorpion*.

The sailors took turns to be the officer on watch – always scanning the horizon for enemy ships – always knowing they could be attacked at any moment. Keith Langton recalled how they felt. "The fact that we were always wet was incredibly depressing; it helped the cold to bite right through us. We never had time even to change our soggy clothes because 'Action Stations' was called so regularly – often we were on duty more than twenty-two hours a day."

The crew were exhausted, and their conditions are hard to imagine today. As Langton said, they "had to avoid touching any metal surfaces or railings on the *Scorpion*. Anyone careless enough to do so would get a severe burn from the frozen metal which would stick to their fingers and cause terrible pain." The resulting burns had to be treated by the ship's doctor.

But by 1942, the Allies had one great advantage in the war. Code-breakers back in Britain had finally managed to crack the German radio codes for orders sent out to their U-boats, surface ships and air force. That meant the *Scorpion* was well informed about the position of the enemy. But the men on board were constantly listening out for the buzz of a German spotter plane overhead, looking for them. If they heard one, they knew that an attack would soon follow.

Another German tactic involved their U-boats. These would form a line in front of a British convoy. In order to get past, the warships in the convoy had to fire at them.

Then the convoy tried to charge through the line. On one occasion, the British code-breakers let the convoy down. They failed to decode an important enemy message. The sailors on the *Scorpion,* and the other warships in the convoy, didn't know that the German warships *Admiral Hipper* and *Lützow* had put to sea, along with six destroyers.

As Langton remembered it, visibility was very poor that day. "All I could see was shifting mist with dense patches of fog in it ... I stood in a completely soundless world and the *Scorpion* seemed smothered in a deep blanket."

It must have been uncanny. The usual intense cold meant that icicles were hanging from the ship's guns.

Suddenly, without warning and without the sounding of 'Action Stations' on the ships, the German fleet attacked the convoy. Within minutes one of the *Scorpion*'s sister ships was fired on by a German destroyer. Instructions were shouted for the *Scorpion* to counter-attack.

All the British destroyers moved forward to fight the German ships. Four times the German ship, the *Admiral Hipper*, tried to break through the destroyers' defences to fire on the convoy; four times she was forced back. Then snow started to fall.

Soon the battle was taking place in the middle of a snowstorm, which helped the British at first. But then an eight-inch shell fired by the *Admiral Hipper* hit one of the British ships, HMS *Onslow,* causing severe damage and heavy casualties. Another of the convoy's destroyers, HMS *Achates*, and a minesweeper – HMS *Bramble* – were also sunk.

But the enemy suffered too. The *Admiral Hipper* was hit more than once, and retreated into the snowstorm. Oddly, the *Lützow* never opened fire, despite being in a good position to cause major damage to the convoy. Another German destroyer was sunk by the convoy's warships, and finally the convoy continued on its way.

In fact, the Commander of the German navy, Grand Admiral Raeder, was forced to resign in disgrace after the battle of Barents Sea. He was replaced by Admiral Karl Doenitz (right), a former U-boat commander. Doenitz was a very good commander. With this capable opponent in place, the war at sea became even more dangerous for the Allies.

The convoys' route usually ran between Scotland and Iceland, and then on to Murmansk in Russia (see the map on page 15). By 1943 the biggest threat to British convoys came from the German battleship *Scharnhorst*. On Christmas Day 1943, Keith Langton's captain discovered that this

powerful battleship had slipped out of her
hiding place in a Norwegian fjord,
accompanied by five destroyers. The
German commander was determined to
save the reputation of his navy by
attacking the *Scorpion*'s convoy.

Weather conditions in the Arctic were
as grim as ever. But the weather would

slow the *Scharnhorst* down as well as the British convoy. It might even make her more vulnerable to counter-attack.

HMS *Belfast* was the first to spot the *Scharnhorst* on her radar. Then HMS *Norfolk* opened fire and scored a direct hit, but caused little damage. Neither the *Belfast's* nor the *Norfolk's* commanders wanted to attack too hard. That would make the *Scharnhorst* run for cover. The monster had to be lured as far away from port as possible.

Joined by HMS *Sheffield*, the British fleet pounded the German battleship with their guns. Then the *Scharnhorst* ran straight into an ambush led by HMS *Duke of York*. The *Scorpion* was nearby, ready to play her part.

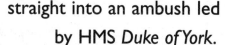

The *Duke of York* opened fire with her
powerful 14-inch guns. The *Scharnhorst*
was badly damaged and headed east, but
she no longer had the speed to outdistance
the British destroyers.

They torpedoed the *Scharnhorst* time and time again. Finally, at 7.45 a.m., there was an enormous explosion, and she sank. Keith Langton saw some survivors from the *Scharnhorst* struggling in the bitterly cold sea, covered in oil, choking and freezing.

The British ships tried to rescue all the survivors they could. But of the *Scharnhorst*'s crew of two thousand men, only thirty-six men survived. With the sinking of the *Scharnhorst*, Germany's navy had suffered a significant defeat.

Despite the continuing presence of U-boats lurking among the icebergs, and aeroplanes patrolling the skies, the Allied convoys continued. The *Scorpion* successfully escorted nine British convoys. Keith Langton, that young midshipman, must have been proud to have helped win the war at sea in such difficult conditions.

# X-CRAFT
# ATTACK

*The three Royal Navy submarines towed their midget submarines towards the Norwegian fjord where the huge German warships sheltered. There was a slight hum from the submarines' engines, but that was kept as quiet as possible, so as not to alert the enemy to the impending attack. If the daring plan worked, the battleships that posed such a threat to Britain's Arctic convoys would be destroyed.*

The Admiralty ran the Royal Navy. It was very worried about the threat to the Arctic

convoys from three German battleships –
*Tirpitz*, *Lützow* and *Scharnhorst*.

The Commander of the German navy
was Admiral Doenitz. He knew how
important the three big ships were.

He had hidden them away from attack in the Norwegian fjords. There his dangerous monsters lay, safe in their hiding place from attack by ships of the Royal Navy.

*The location of Alten Fjord in northern Norway.*

The narrowness of the Norwegian fjords (deep inlets) gave the battleships their main protection. In addition, Alten Fjord – in northern Norway – was too far from any Allied base for an aerial attack. Bombers of the RAF could have reached the fjords, but they would have needed to carry extra fuel for the journey. That would have reduced their bomb load. The waters of the fjords were heavily mined, so any Allied ship trying to enter would have been blown up, or caught in the huge nets set to catch submarines – like fish in a fisherman's net.

The threat from the three battleships had been endlessly discussed by the Allies. Some convoy sailings had been cancelled when British intelligence learned that these German warships were going to sea. But then a daring plan was developed. The Allies decided to go in and attack the German battleships where they lay in harbour. And they would use an amazing new development – miniature submarines.

Experimental work on midget submarines began in 1941. The prototype X-craft weighed only thirty-five tonnes, with an overall length of nearly sixteen metres. Each sub carried a crew of four. Space inside the tiny craft was very restricted. The crew got fresh air whenever they could by bringing the submarines to the surface, and getting out on to the deck.

The Royal Navy took delivery of the new X-craft in January 1943 and crews began training straight away for their dangerous mission. Every little submarine carried two detachable charges with their fuses on a timer. Each charge contained two tonnes of Armatex explosive. These were to be placed on the seabed, directly beneath the enemy ships.

The midget submarines could not make the voyage to Norway under their own power. That was beyond their capabilities, for their targets were nearly 3,000 kilometres away. So, on 11 September 1943, six full-sized submarines started towing the X-craft from Scotland to Norway.

The operation was planned for the night of 20 September 1943. There wasn't much time to get everything in place, and launch the daring attack on the German ships.

There were problems from the start. Two of the X-craft broke loose from their 'parent' submarines during the voyage, and were lost. The other four all reached the Norwegian coast, but the extent of the plan had to be cut back.

The original idea had been ambitious, with attacks planned on all three German battleships. But because two midget submarines had been lost, that target had to be reduced. Then a third midget submarine developed mechanical problems. It had to be abandoned at the entrance to Alten Fjord. Now only three X-craft were available, and so the mission had to be adapted to this new situation. The commanders decided to use the remaining three X-craft to attack just one of the German ships: the *Tirpitz*.

The crew of the three surviving X-craft, X5, X6 and X7, made their way carefully around the minefield at the entrance to Alten Fjord. They met up in the shadow of an island, soon after midnight. The *Tirpitz* was now only nine kilometres away, but the voyage was still difficult and dangerous. Lieutenant Godfrey Place commanded X7. His miniature submarine got caught in the German nets. He just managed to free her, with great difficulty. Then another X-craft was caught in the nets, but once again the crew managed to wrench her free.

The crew of X7 stopped her motor and let her rise silently to the surface. Lieutenant Place described what happened next. "When she broke surface I saw we were inside the close-net defences – how we got underneath I have no idea – about thirty metres from the *Tirpitz*'s port [left side] beam ."

In this ideal position, Place and his crew were able to drop both their charges under

different parts of the *Tirpitz*. As he recalled:
"It was just as we were letting go the
second charge that we heard the first signs
of enemy counter-attack – but, oddly
enough, we were wrong in assuming they
were meant for us."

Lieutenant Place tried to retrace his course, aiming for the place where the submarine had managed to slip in under the net. He tried again and again, but he couldn't find an escape route through the net and out of the fjord. The crew couldn't raise the X-craft's magnetic compass, in case it caught in the net. Place then tried to use a course indicator (a compass that remains steady during alterations of direction, and shows a vessel's true position).  But the noise it made was so loud that Place thought it might give their position away, and he switched it off again.

The crew of X7 were getting desperate. "We tried most places along the bottom of those nets, passing under the *Tirpitz* more than once, and even breaking surface at times, but nowhere could we find a way through." Time was running out.

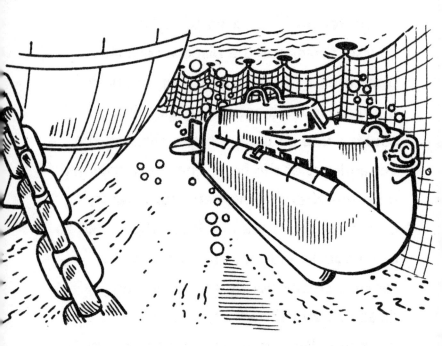

Place gave the order for the submarine to dive to the bottom of the fjord. He knew he had to put as much distance as possible between his craft and the expected explosion of the *Tirpitz*. But before the submarine had time to dive, the explosion came – a continuous roar that seemed to last for a long time.

Ever since they had dropped their charges, Place had known that X7 could be blown to pieces at any moment. But when the explosion died away, he was surprised to find his submarine completely intact, although slightly damaged. If only he could find that space underneath the net! Then X7 could slip through it, and escape undetected. But despite more frantic searching, Lieutenant Place could not find a way out.

The X7 was already being fired on, and the commander knew he had to surrender. They would be in very serious trouble with the Germans, for blowing up one of their most important battleships.

Place remembered bringing X7 to the surface, and opening the fore hatch, "just enough to allow the waving of a white sweater". The firing stopped immediately, so Place said he then "came outside and waved the sweater more vigorously".

Then the midget submarine swung round, and hit an obstruction. Her bow dipped, water poured through the open hatch, and the X-craft began to sink. Lieutenant Place jumped into the water and swam for the shore, calling to his crew to follow.

By the time X7 sank, Place had reached the beach, and stood waving his white sweater in surrender. He still hoped his crew would follow him and be saved. But it was

hard to move fast inside the midget submarine. It was harder still to get out of the top hatch in choppy seas.

The X7 design and the weather, rather than German guns, were too much for the crew of X7. The men struggled desperately to get out, but only one succeeded. All the others drowned, while Place watched from the beach, dismayed and helpless.

Midget submarine X6 was commanded by Lieutenant Donald Cameron. X6 also started to sink once she had released her charges, but her commander and crew all managed to make it to the surface. Later, Place and Cameron realised that X5 must have been sunk by shell fire and depth charges. There were no X5 survivors.

The *Tirpitz* was badly damaged. All three of the battleship's engines had been hit. Hundreds of tonnes of water had poured into her hull. The rudders and steering gear had also been damaged. A massive amount of repair work would have to be done before the crippled *Tirpitz* was seaworthy again. (In fact, she was put out of action until April 1944.) Admiral Doenitz and Hitler were furious.

Despite the loss of life on the British side, the mission was judged a success. The German navy had suffered a heavy blow, and a major threat to the safety of the convoys had been removed.

The midget submarines had been valuable, but their success was mainly due to the initiative and bravery of the crews. Place and Cameron, the surviving commanders, were both awarded the Victoria Cross medal – Britain's highest award for courage under fire.

# AMPHIBIOUS WARFARE

*The Gallipoli campaign was one of the most tragic mistakes of the First World War (1914-18). In 1915, the Allies (Britain and the countries of the British Empire, together with France and Russia) declared war on Turkey. Allied troops landed at Gallipoli, in Turkey. They aimed to defeat the Turks and march on the Turkish capital, Constantinople (now called Istanbul). But the Gallipoli landings were a disaster.*

British, Australian and New Zealand soldiers died in their thousands. The men were killed on the beaches near their landing sites. They couldn't move quickly from their ships to the shore, and then into enemy territory. They got caught in a bottleneck as they left the ships, and made an easy target for the Turkish guns.

In 1921, when the war was over, an American army major called Earl Ellis developed a better plan for ship-to-shore transport. Ellis wanted army leaders to learn from the Gallipoli campaign's mistakes. His plan became a model for amphibious (sea-to-shore) warfare in the Pacific, during the next war. Ellis realised that troops must be carefully trained. He said that Marines – tough soldiers who could fight both at sea and on land – would make the best possible task force.

In 1933, the US Marine Corps began to try out amphibious vehicles – ones that could operate both at sea and on land. The new vehicles also had to give troops protection from enemy fire. Engineers were still struggling to meet all the Marines' needs when a boat builder, Andrew Higgins of New Orleans, contacted the US government. Higgins had developed a vessel for crossing rivers. His craft was easy to land, and it could also be pulled back into the water quickly. It seemed ideal.

The US government had to admit that the Higgins landing craft design was much better than the Marines' prototype. The US Navy didn't buy Higgins' invention, but his design was used in the development of the landing craft used in the Second World War.

The use of amphibious craft did not start in Britain until 1937. Then, the British army leaders decided that several brigades of Royal Marines must be trained to take part in amphibious landings. A top group of Royal Marine soldiers, known as commandos, were chosen for this special training. The Marines were taught to carry out top secret and highly dangerous missions. They learned hand-to-hand fighting, and to use explosives. They also learned how to launch an attack from landing craft.

Then the Inter-Service Training and Development Centre was set up in Portsmouth. The centre developed a plan for amphibious warfare that involved all the armed forces.

The Royal Marines' new role not only included using amphibious landing craft to land troops in an invasion. It also covered offloading or retrieving vital armaments that would otherwise be abandoned, if an invasion went wrong.

The first commando raid of the Second World War took place on 27 February 1942. It was called 'Operation Biting'. This was an attack on a German radar station at Bruneval, on the coast of occupied France. The raid took place to capture German radar equipment. This top secret operation involved 120 men from C Company, the Second Battalion of the First Parachute

Brigade. It was under the command of
Major John Frost. The commandos were
to be dropped from RAF aircraft, and then
capture the radar equipment. The men
would have to make their way to the nearby
beach. There they would be picked up by a
flotilla of six landing craft.

On the night, everything went more or less to plan. Royal Navy destroyers and a squadron of RAF Spitfire aircraft escorted the successful commandos back to Portsmouth. It might have been a small operation, but it was an important one. It would not have been possible without the use of landing craft. Now the commandos had proved that the new amphibious landing craft could make a major contribution to winning the war.

After the evacuation of the British Expeditionary Force from Dunkirk in 1940, the Allied commanders realised that a massive invasion of Nazi-occupied France would have to take place. To do that, tanks and other armoured vehicles must be landed on the French beaches.

So the British Prime Minister, Winston Churchill, ordered the development of a new kind of landing craft. This was known as the Landing Ship Tank, or LST.

The prototype LST could carry twenty tanks or thirty-three lorries, but it couldn't come close into the shore. A better design was badly needed, but most of the experienced British engineers were fighting in the war. Without their skill, the right design could not be developed and produced in the British shipyards. But when the United States joined the Allies on 7 December 1941, Churchill discovered that American shipyards were prepared to carry out the contract for a better LST. That was excellent news!

The first of the new landing-craft designs was ready by 20 September 1942. Before the war ended, 1,050 tank-carrying landing craft were built by the Americans.

Although versatile landing craft were

available by 1942, a successful invasion of Europe was still a long way off. The first attempt in August 1942, at Dieppe on the French coast, was a disaster. The plan had been to land 5,000 soldiers on the beaches, east and west of the town. They were to be supported by 1,000 commandos.

But the attack soon ran into major problems. The weather was bad and the campaign's commander, General Montgomery, was needed to lead another

campaign. The British government wanted to avoid killing French civilians, so the planned heavy aerial bombardment of Dieppe was abandoned. Then British Intelligence – the spy network – discovered that the German High Command had learned details of the invasion. Alarmed, Montgomery recommended that the plan should be abandoned. But Churchill and Vice-Admiral Mountbatten had planned the Dieppe raid. They ignored his advice.

The naval force of light ships and landing craft was made up of 237 vessels. The fleet sailed from Portsmouth, Shoreham and Newhaven on 18 August 1942. Royal Navy minesweepers had cleared a passage through the English Channel. That helped the fleet to get through a gap in the German minefields.

One of the groups of vessels then met a German convoy. The ships exchanged fire, so the German coastal defences were alerted. When the landing craft got to the beaches at Dieppe they met a wall of heavy enemy fire. The escorting destroyers fired back, but they didn't have enough power to knock the

German defenders out of action. Then the troops on the landing craft came under attack from German bombers. Many of the Allied soldiers, most of whom were Canadian, were mown down as they landed.

After that, the Allies' only hope lay in their tanks. They could have taken over Dieppe's narrow streets and destroyed enemy defences. But none of the tanks was able to climb the high ridges of shingle on the beaches at the sea front.

The order was given to withdraw. But because the battalion commanders (who would usually have made sure the orders were carried out) were amongst the casualties, the situation was chaotic. No one knew what they were supposed to do.

Lieutenant Colonel Charles Merritt remembered the disaster well. "I was shocked at the sight on the beach. Instead of finding a few scattered remnants still hanging back, the place was swarming with men, hundreds of them. That was my mistake. I should have gone down much earlier to ensure they were re-embarking as they reached the beach."

A lack of experience meant that the soldiers didn't get back to the safety of their ships quickly enough. More than 5,000 of the original 6,000 troops landed were killed, wounded or captured.

Another survivor of the disaster was Lieutenant David Flory, who was in command of one of the landing craft. He recalled what happened. "I proceeded to the beach which lay under a thick smokescreen and ... found the men swimming out from the beaches to get away from the machine-gunning ... There were some corpses in the water; those that were alive had little strength left. I picked up about twenty men from the water ... By this time one engine was not working and the steering apparatus was defective."

Despite his damaged craft, Lieutenant Flory tried to rescue every man he could. Some troops waded a hundred metres out from the beach into the sea, and struggled desperately, under heavy machine-gun fire, to board Lieutenant Flory's craft.

The steering improved enough for
Flory to put to sea, and escape the enemy
bombardment. But the number of soldiers
who survived the attack was small.

Although many soldiers were killed at
Dieppe, important lessons *were* learned.
Now it was clear
that enemy guns
had to be
destroyed by
heavy aerial
bombardment
before an attack
took place. It was
also essential
to choose
the right place
to land, far
from well-
defended towns.

The last piece of the jigsaw was the invention of "Mulberry". This was the Allies' own prefabricated harbour. It could be towed into position by the navy, and the invading troops could easily be supplied with provisions and weapons.

By June 1944, the Allies were finally ready to invade Europe. Because of these improvements, an enormous number of men and armaments were successfully landed on the Normandy beaches on D-Day. The Allied soldiers who began the invasion of German-occupied France gradually took the countries of Europe back from Nazi control.

So the landings turned the tide of the war, and led to the German surrender in 1945. The amphibious craft developed by the Allies were a vital part of the strategy that finally won the war.

# DEFEAT AT LEYTE GULF

*While Allied sailors watched in horror, the survivors of a wrecked Japanese ship tried to drown themselves or cut their own throats. Deeply shocked, the Allies realised that most officers and sailors in the Japanese navy would rather kill themselves than be taken prisoner. In Japanese culture, surrender was seen as an act of cowardice. It brought deep dishonour.*

In November 1938 the Japanese Prime Minister, Prince Fumimaro Konoe, announced a new foreign policy for Japan. He called it a 'New Order for East Asia'.

The 'New Order' plan brought both Korea and Manchuria under full Japanese control. But Europe and the USA did not want Japan to have military and economic control of any more of South-East Asia.

*Many Second World War battles were fought around the Philippine Islands, in this part of the Pacific Ocean.*

Beijing

CHINA

INDIA

BURMA

JAPAN

Tokyo

PHILIPPINE
ISLANDS

Saigon

LEYTE
GULF

Singapore

BORNEO

JAVA

NEW GUINEA

AUSTRALIA

The Second World War began in Europe in 1939, between the Allies and Germany. Japan knew that while that was going on, France and Britain would not be able to defend their territories in the far east. That gave Japan an opportunity to expand. The USA also had territories and economic interests in the Pacific. If they could be driven out too, Japan believed it could dominate the whole Pacific region.

In December 1941, the Japanese air force made a surprise attack on the American fleet at Pearl Harbor. The bombing was highly successful. A total of 18 warships and 187 aircraft were destroyed and 2,400 servicemen were killed in the two-hour attack. But the raid had serious long-term effects. It provoked the USA into declaring war on Japan and joining the Allies in the war against Germany.

The Japanese belief in their 'New Order' for South-East Asia was firmly rooted in their religious and cultural traditions. So was their belief in the importance of honour above human life. The Japanese leaders ignored America's massive fighting resources. The possibility of total defeat for Japan was not considered.

That was a serious mistake. By 1944, Japanese forces had lost control of most of the Pacific. Many Japanese ships had been sunk by American submarines. They could not replace the lost ships, because supplies of ship-building materials could not get through the Allied blockade. Most of the tankers that brought oil from the Philippines to Japan had been destroyed or damaged by the Allies. Oil reserves were fast running out. Soon, Japan would have no fuel for their battleships and air force.

The Americans prepared to attack the Philippines in the autumn of 1944. Japan got ready for a final sea battle with the American navy. Even with the reduced Japanese fleet, there was a chance of victory. If Japan won the battle, they might be able to take control of the war again. But if they lost, the Japanese commanders knew that the Americans would take the Philippines. An American victory would mean no more oil supplies for Japan. With no fuel, they would face total defeat.

Admiral Toyoda was in overall command of the Japanese defence of the Philippines. He described the problem in brutally frank terms. "If the worst should happen, there was a chance that we would lose the entire fleet; but we felt that the chance had to be taken. There would be no sense in saving the fleet at the expense of the loss of the Philippines."

Admiral Toyoda was right. The fleet would be no use to Japan if they lost the Philippines – because they would be cut off from their vital fuel supply.

Many ships in the Japanese fleet were out of action. Japan had only four surviving operational aircraft carriers, based on the island of Formosa. They had hardly enough aircraft to fill a quarter of their hangar space. There were only a couple of battleships left, some light cruisers, and a few destroyers.

Toyoda decided to use the rest of his carrier fleet (under Vice Admiral Ozama) as a decoy. This action was designed to lure most of the US Navy away from

the Philippines. Once the Americans had
been tricked in that way, the Japanese
could attack the Philippines from the sea.
The attack centred on Leyte, a small
island in the Philippines group.

The operation began badly for the
Japanese. One section of their fleet –

which was to launch the attack on Leyte —
was attacked by American submarines
before the ships reached their destination.
So the strength of the Japanese attack was
already blunted. Now, instead of being lured
away, the Americans knew that Japanese
ships were in the Leyte Gulf.

But in this first battle, land-based
Japanese bombers backed up the Japanese
ships. The US carrier *Princeton* was sunk. But

then American aircraft sank the Japanese ship *Musashi*, one of the largest carriers ever built.

American planes also attacked the huge Japanese battleship *Yamato*. They could only make a dent in her armour plating, because the battleship was so tough. One American bomber pilot remembered that attack. "I had never seen either of the two Japanese super-battleships before. They were massive – and looked totally unsinkable. In some strange way I also saw them as metal monsters that would survive whatever we threw at them."

Both sides opened fire. An American pilot who took part in the attack on the *Musashi* recalled seeing "... the most amazing patterns of pink and white and purple with silver phosphorous balls spilling from the centre of each shell burst." Then the

American bombers dropped their bombs.
There were many underwater explosions.
The *Musashi* was battered and holed, but
the crew wouldn't surrender. At that point
the young pilot realised "... that the whole
[Japanese] nation was prepared to die with

honour rather than to escape or surrender.
... Later the *Musashi*'s engine started up, but
she didn't steam away.

She remained where she was, firing back, taking the punishment as torpedo bombers from another five US carriers tore their way into her hull. At 7.33 p. m. she suddenly began to roll over and sink."

The sinking of the *Musashi* marked the beginning of the end for the Japanese fleet.

By midnight on 24 October 1944 the southern flank of the Japanese navy, under Admiral Nishimura, was in position. In this second battle of Leyte Gulf, two Japanese battleships and a heavy cruiser formed a line. Lighter cruisers and destroyers were on their left flank. Admiral Nishimura knew the line of Japanese ships would be met by six American battleships. But he also knew the Americans had a bad record for fighting at night.

The night was dark and calm. There was no moon, and the sea was glassy. The American destroyers attacked, and the Japanese ships fired back. On board the *Yamashiro*, Admiral Nishimura sailed on. He did not yet know that one of his battleships had been hit. But a few minutes later, two divisions of American destroyers, hugging the dark shores of the island, prepared for a second attack.

Admiral Nishimura suddenly realised that he was witnessing a disaster. One of his battleships had been destroyed, a destroyer had been blown up, and his own flagship had been hit. American night-fighting tactics had improved enormously. The American attack on Nishimura's fleet was both overwhelming and relentless.

A British sailor remembered that October night in 1944. "At the time, I was on the upper deck of the HMS *Shropshire* to witness these early salvos from the *Yamashiro*'s 14-inch guns, which were to pass over the *Shropshire* and which, to me, sounded like controlled thunder." The *Yamashiro* was repeatedly hit by the 16-inch shells of the American battleships *West Virginia* and the 14-inch shells of the *Tennessee* and the *California*. The American ships were all equipped with the most up-

to-date fire-control system (the controls
that aimed the guns). That made for
devastatingly accurate shooting.

To those on duty, the scene was extraordinary. The American ships kept up a huge barrage of fire, and the cruisers carried tracer ammunition that left a smoke trail in its wake. The battleship *Yamashiro* was on fire from bow to stern, and burning fiercely. That was made worse when the ship was hit by a further two torpedoes from the destroyer *Newcomb*.

At approximately 4.20 a.m. the *Yamashiro* finally sank. The heavy cruiser *Mogami* and

the destroyer *Shigure* were both badly damaged and retreated. The second Battle of Leyte Gulf had been overwhelmingly won by the US Navy.

Japanese Vice Admiral Ozama was still trying to use his aircraft carriers as bait to draw the Americans north. But despite his efforts, the American fleet at first seemed to ignore his presence. Eventually, the American Commander-in-Chief, Admiral Halsey, went into action. This became the third Battle of Leyte Gulf.

Halsey was later severely criticised for having left the main battle area without informing anyone. But he was successful in completely destroying all that remained of Japan's once-mighty naval power.

The three separate but linked battles of Leyte Gulf confirmed American naval supremacy in the Pacific.

But these battles also showed how determined the Japanese were, even in defeat. Japanese forces would fight to the death, even when the odds were heavily stacked against them. They would not retreat from an enemy. Their code of honour was a rigid and demanding one. No Japanese commander could easily consider surrender. To surrender was thought to insult the Emperor, and the Japanese people.

# GLOSSARY

## Allies

*Countries such as Britain, France and the USA that fought together against Germany, Japan, Italy and some other countries during World War Two.*

## Blockade

*When a navy patrols an enemy's coastline and sinks ships to prevent vital supplies from getting through.*

## Destroyer

*A fast warship armed with both guns and torpedoes for sinking enemy vessels.*

## D-Day

*Officially named "Operation Overlord". D-Day was 6 June 1944, when the Allies landed in France to begin freeing Europe from Nazi occupation.*

## Dictator

*A leader who imposes his will on a country using military force and intimidation instead of elections.*

# Fjord

The Scandinavian word for a bay, or inlet. It literally means a place where the land meets the water.

# Landing craft

A flat-bottomed ship for landing troops on a beach. The Landing Ship Tank, or LST, was developed during the Second World War to help with the invasion of occupied France by the Allies.

# Nazi

A member of Adolf Hitler's National Socialist Party and supporter of its policies.

# U-Boat

U-Boat is a translation from the German of "U-boot". It is short for "Unterseeboot" or an undersea boat.

# USSR

The Union of Soviet Socialist Republics, often referred to as "Soviet Russia" or the "Soviet Union".

# WAR AT SEA

*The enemy was all around. The Luftwaffe (the German air force), the U-boats and the warships of the German navy all lay in wait. And there were always the icebergs, and the freezing fog, of the Barents Sea.*

# WAR ON LAND

*The first wave of troops was mostly killed, cut down as they came ashore. Then the second wave of troops had to advance over the bodies of the dead. Survival was their main instinct.*

# WAR AT HOME

*The boys had a meeting and decided to take as many knives and forks as they could get their hands on in order to defend themselves. But they realised that knives and forks would be little use against the Nazis' guns.*

# WAR IN THE AIR

*Dundas's Spitfire began to spiral downwards, spinning wildly while he pulled and wrenched and hammered at the hood to open it. But Dundas still couldn't get the canopy open wide enough to escape through the gap.*